L.S.C.A. Title I

Project YOUTHREAC.

S0-BCA-576

The Young Scientist Investigates

Pond Life

by
Terry Jennings

CHILDRENS PRESS®

CHICAGO

Library of Congress Cataloging-in-Publication Data

Jennings, Terry J.
    Pond life / by Terry Jennings.
       p.   cm. — (The Young scientist investigates.)
    Includes index.
    Summary: An introduction to the plant and animal life of
ponds which includes study questions, activities, and
experiments.
    ISBN 0-516-08406-2
    1. Pond ecology—Juvenile literature. [1. Pond animals. 2. Pond
plants.] I. Title. II. Series: Jennings, Terry J. Young scientist
investigates.
    QH541.5.P63J46   1988
    574.5′26322—dc 19   88-22880
                                             CIP
                                             AC

North American edition published in 1989 by Regensteiner
Publishing Enterprises, Inc.

© Terry Jennings 1985
First published 1985 by Oxford University Press

Printed in the United States of America
1 2 3 4 5 6 7 8 9 10 R 98 97 96 95 94 93 92 91 90 89

The Young Scientist Investigates

Pond Life

Contents

Ponds

There are ponds almost everywhere. There are ponds in yards, parks, farms, and city squares. Some ponds occur high on hills and mountains.

Natural ponds were often made when hollows in the ground filled with rainwater. For these hollows to hold water there had to be clay or another rock underneath the ground to stop the water from soaking away. A few ponds were formed when a river changed its course. But most ponds were made by people. In days gone by, almost all villages and farms had at least one pond where horses and cattle could drink. Many of these ponds were simply holes dug in the ground and lined with clay. Some larger ponds were made when rain filled abandoned gravel pits and clay pits. Modern ponds in yards and parks are usually lined with concrete or plastic.

All ponds have water that is still. Only the wind ripples the surface. Usually the pond is shallow enough for sunlight to reach the bottom. This allows plants to grow in the water. As we shall see later, ponds are the homes of many wild creatures.

Changing ponds

Some ponds are large enough to be used for boating and sailing. Other ponds are small. There is no real difference between a pond and a lake. A lake is generally large, while a pond is small. Some ponds are heavily shaded by trees. Others are right out in the open. The ponds which are out in the open have the most wild life in them.

Ponds are always changing. The level of water in ponds may change a great deal. During and after heavy rain a pond may fill to overflowing. Ponds also fill when the winter snows melt. In hot summer weather a pond may lose water to the air. The water goes into the air as the invisible gas water vapor. We say the water has evaporated.

Ponds which last only a short time and then dry up are temporary ponds. Temporary ponds have few animals and plants living in them. Ponds which always have water in them are called permanent ponds. Permanent ponds are homes for many kinds of wildlife.

A mountain lake

A pond shaded by trees

A town pond used by fishermen

A temporary pond

Pond plants

Permanent ponds, which receive plenty of sunlight, have many plants growing in them. Often tiny water plants, called algae, cover the mud with a green film. Some of these algae are so small they can only be seen with a microscope. Other algae look like a mass of green cotton wool.

Water weeds are also abundant in sunny ponds. Some, such as duckweed and waterfern, are small and float on the surface. Others are rooted in the bottom of the pond. Pondweed and water milfoil grow completely underwater. Water crowfoot, snakeweed, and arrowhead have some leaves below water and some above the surface. Water lilies have only floating leaves.

Open ponds usually have a fringe of plants. These include rushes, cattails, reeds, meadowsweet, purple loosestrife, bur reed, forget-me-nots, and water plantains, The muddy ground around the pond has sedges, rushes, grasses, and marsh marigold. Trees such as alder, gray poplar and willows may also grow around the pond.

If the pond is not kept clean, it may become filled with mud and overgrown with plants. Then it slowly turns into a swamp. After many years it may become woodland.

1. Bur reeds. 2. Cattail. 3. Reeds. 4. Water plantain. 5. Arrowhead. 6. Forget-me-not. 7. Marsh marigold. 8. Water lily. 9. Duckweed. 10. Water crowfoot. 11. Snakeweed. *Inset.* Algae, highly magnified.

Small water animals

Many small animals live in ponds. Some are so tiny that they can be seen only with a microscope. They feed on bacteria and the smallest algae in the water. Water fleas, freshwater sponges, and mussels sift algae from the water. Many animals feed on the larger plants. Mayfly nymphs, water snails, and newly-hatched frog and toad tadpoles feed on plants. So do water voles, or water rats as they are sometimes wrongly called.

Animals which feed on plant material are called herbivores. Herbivores are, in turn, food for other larger, fiercer animals. These fierce animals are called carnivores. The carnivores in a pond include water beetles, water spiders, dragonfly and damselfly nymphs, water striders and sticklebacks.

The lives of the plants and animals in a pond are linked together in what are called food chains. All food chains begin with plants. These plants are eaten by herbivores. The herbivores are food for carnivores.

A water flea with eggs

A freshwater shrimp

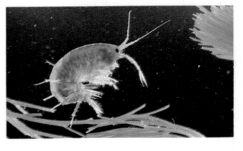

A water vole

Two pond food chains (not to scale)

algae   water flea   stickleback   pike

As well as the herbivores and carnivores, some of the animals in a pond are scavengers. They eat dead leaves, dead animals, and the droppings of animals. They help to keep the pond clean. Water striders, sludge worms, and freshwater shrimps are scavengers. Scavengers also provide food for the carnivores in the pond.

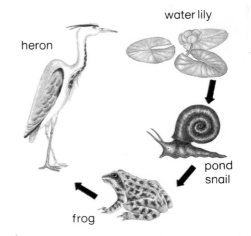

heron   water lily   pond snail   frog

Fish

Goldfish

A mirror carp

A tench

A male stickleback and nest

Many ponds have fish in them. Ponds in parks or gardens may be a home for goldfish. Other ponds may have fish such as carp, tench, roach, and perch. These fish are sometimes put in ponds for fishermen to catch. Most pond fishes are rounder and fatter than those that live in streams and fast-flowing rivers. Generally pond fish swim more slowly too.

One of the most common pond fishes is the stickleback or tiddler. Sometimes these little fish are put in ponds to eat the larvae of mosquitoes. They also eat worms, insects, and small fish.

In the spring the male stickleback develops a red throat and belly. He builds a small nest made from pieces of water plants stuck together. The male stickleback then does a strange zig-zag dance through the water. He hopes that this will attract a female. When a female stickleback has laid her eggs in the nest, the male drives her away. He then fans the eggs with his fins. This keeps fresh water containing dissolved oxygen passing over the eggs. When the eggs hatch, the male guards the baby fish. Eventually the baby sticklebacks are large enough to fend for themselves. Then they swim away from the nest for good.

Some common water birds

Most of the water birds can be seen all year-round. The moorhen is common on many ponds, large and small. There it feeds on water plants and small water animals. The moorhen's feathers are mainly black. Its beak is bright red and it has a white patch under its short tail.

The moorhen's nest is made of dead water plants. It is often built amongst living rushes or reeds. In the nest the hen moorhen lays between 5 and 11 speckled eggs. Baby moorhens are black and fluffy. They can swim soon after they have hatched.

Another common water bird in larger ponds is the coot. Like the moorhen, the coot has black feathers. But the coot is bigger than the moorhen and has a white forehead and beak. The large toes of the coot have loose skin or lobes along the sides. They allow the coot to swim well and also to walk across mud without sinking in. The coot feeds on water plants and small water animals.

Moorhen on its nest

A kingfisher with a stickleback

A heron

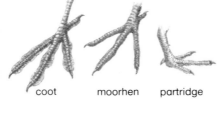
coot   moorhen   partridge

Left, a coot

Less common are kingfishers and herons. These birds sometimes visit ponds, even those in gardens, to catch fish. The heron also catches water voles and frogs at the water's edge.

Ducks and swans

Mallard duck with young, drake *inset*

Tufted duck and drake

Several kinds of ducks visit ponds. The most common is the mallard. The male or drake mallard has a dark green head and white collar. The female or duck mallard is a dull brown.

The mallard nests amongst reeds or under low bushes on the bank. In the nest the duck lays her pale green eggs. Soon after they have hatched, the fluffy ducklings learn to swim. Mallard feed on the surface of the water. There they eat mainly floating water plants together with some insects and water snails.

The tufted duck dives underwater to search for water plants and small water animals. The drake tufted duck has black and white feathers. His mate is mainly brown. All ducks have webbed feet. This means their toes are joined together by skin so that they can swim well.

Swans building their nest *inset* and with their cygnets

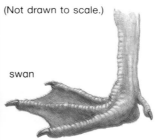

(Not drawn to scale.)

swan

mallard

Swans also have webbed feet. The mute swan lives on ponds in both city and country. The male swan is known as the cob, his mate is called the pen. The pen builds a large nest made of sticks, grass, and reeds. The eggs take nearly 6 weeks to hatch. At first the young swans, or cygnets, are gray in color. They begin to turn white during their first winter.

Ponds in summer and winter

Summer is a busy time in the pond. The weather is warm and the days are long. Plants grow rapidly, flower, and produce their seeds. The plants provide fresh food for the many herbivores. As the herbivores increase in numbers, so do the carnivores that feed on them. With so much food, the animals can breed and feed their young.

By contrast, winter is a difficult time for the pond plants and animals. In really cold weather the pond may freeze over. Fortunately, it is usually only the surface of the water which freezes. Deeper down the temperature of the water rarely falls below 39.2°F.

Water boatmen and a few other smaller pond animals are active throughout the winter. Some others, such as dragonfly and mayfly nymphs, freshwater shrimps, and mussels rest for many weeks. They hide in the mud. Some adult animals, including water fleas, die although their eggs stay alive. Roach, perch, sticklebacks, and pike are among the fishes which remain active throughout the winter. Others such as carp and tench bury themselves in the mud. They remain there until the temperature rises. Most of the plants die. Many of them will send up new shoots when the warmer weather returns. In others, only the seeds remain to grow the next year.

A pond in summer *above* and the same pond in winter *below*

Life in a frozen pond

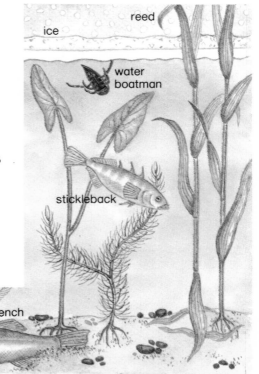

10

Do you remember?

(Look for the answers in the part of the book you have just been reading if you do not know them.)

1   How were many natural ponds made?

2   Why were ponds dug on many farms?

3   What is the water like in ponds?

4   What is the difference between a pond and a lake?

5   What is a temporary pond?

6   What is a permanent pond?

7   What is algae?

8   What may happen if a pond is not kept clean?

9   What do the tiniest animals in a pond feed on?

10   What do we call the animals that feed on plants?

11   What do we call the fierce animals that eat other animals?

12   What is a food chain?

13   What sort of things do the scavengers in a pond eat?

14   What does a male stickleback do to attract a female to his nest?

15   Why does the male stickleback fan the eggs with his fins?

16   How do the large toes of a coot help it?

17   Where does the tufted duck find its food?

18   What names are given to male and female swans?

19   Why do ducks and swans have webbed feet?

20   Which part of a pond freezes first?

Things to do

1   **Studying a pond.** A pond-dipping expedition can be very interesting and fun. *Never* go looking for pond life alone, though. And always push a stick into the water and mud to test the depth before you wade at the edge.

One of the most important things you need is a net. The pictures show you how to make a net from a gravy strainer or from the leg of an old pair of tights.

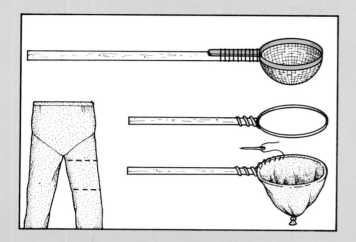

You will also need lots of jars, each tied around the top so as to make a carrying handle. A white plastic tray or pie dish is also very useful. Take a plastic spoon and a small paintbrush to enable you to pick up small animals without damaging them.

Approach the pond quietly or you may see nothing at all when you get there. Carefully sketch the pond. Say how big it is and what the banks are like. What plants are growing around the edges? Make a list of these. What is the bottom of the pond made of: mud, clay, gravel, or sand?

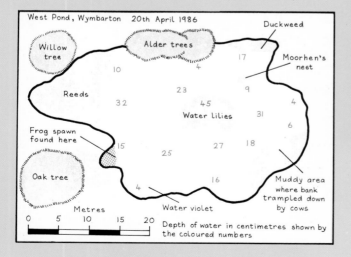

Use the net carefully to search amongst the weeds for animals. Use the net in clear water as well.

After each sweep with your net, empty it into the white tray or dish. Sort your catch into jars containing some pond water and a sprig of water weed.

Only take one or two animals of each kind. Be careful to separate the fierce-looking carnivores in case they eat the other animals you have caught. Put all the rest of the animals back in the pond.

2 Keeping pond animals. You can keep most pond animals for a short time. Use widemouthed containers like those in the picture, so that there is plenty of air in contact with the water.

Put pond water or rainwater in your container with some pieces of water plants. Do not use water straight from the cold water tap. This often has chlorine in it to kill germs. Chlorine will also kill water animals.

You can use tap water if it has been allowed to stand for a day or two to allow the chlorine to escape into the air.

In your container, keep the carnivores separate from the smaller herbivores and scavengers.

Use a magnifying glass to study your pond animals. Answer these questions about each of them.

How big is it?

What color is it?

How many parts does it have to its body?

Does it have wings or wing covers?

Can you see its eyes? What are they like?

How many legs does it have?

What are the legs like?

How does the animal move?

Does it move towards the light (from a window or a flashlight) or away from the light?

What does the animal eat?

How does the animal eat its food?

How does the animal breed?

Does it lay eggs?

Where are the eggs laid and what do they hatch into?

Use books to try to find out the name of the animal. Do not worry if you cannot find out exactly which animal you have. Many pond animals do not have common names. You may have to be content to call your animal an insect, a beetle, a bug, a soft-bodied animal with a shell, or some similar group name.

Be sure you put your animals and plants back in the pond they came from when you have finished with them.

3 Animal foods. As we saw on page 6, some pond animals are herbivores, some are carnivores, and others are scavengers. There is a fourth group of feeders: animals which eat both plants and animals are called omnivores. We humans are omnivores.

Make a table like the one below. Write in the names of as many pond animals as you can in the proper columns. Use this book and other reference books to help you.

Herbivores	Carnivores	Scavengers	Omnivores
Pond snail	Stickleback	Water slater	Tufted duck

4 Food chains. Collect pictures of pond plants and animals. Arrange them in order so that they form food chains which you might find in a pond. Stick your pictures of food chains on a large sheet of paper or card. Join them together by arrows.

Can you think of any ways in which people might form part of a pond food chain?

What is the longest food chain you can make with your pictures?

How many food chains can you think of which might begin with either a water lily or with pondweed?

13

5 How fish breathe. A fish breathes using its mouth and gills. The gills are under the covers at the sides of the fish's head behind its eyes. The fish takes water in through its mouth, and passes it out over its gills, after removing dissolved oxygen from the water.

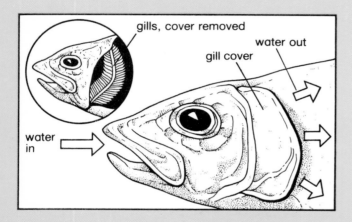

Watch a fish in an aquarium. How many times a minute does the fish open and close its mouth and gill covers? If you tap on the glass gently, does the fish breathe faster or slower?

6 Water and dissolved air. Take a clean jam jar and put some cold water in it. Let the jar warm up by placing it near a radiator or on a sunny windowsill. Can you see tiny bubbles of air rising in the water? This air was dissolved in the water but comes out when you heat the water. Fish use their gills to take in the air's oxygen that has been dissolved in water. Other water animals also breathe this dissolved air to obtain the oxygen it contains.

7 Oxygen in water. All animals must have the gas called oxygen if they are to stay alive. Some water animals get their oxygen from the air at the surface. But as we shall see, water plants also give off oxygen when they make their food. Plants need sunlight to make food and to produce oxygen.

Try the experiment shown in the picture. Put some water weed in the jar of water. If you cannot get any water weed, a piece of garden mint plant will do (wild mint plants grow in and near ponds).

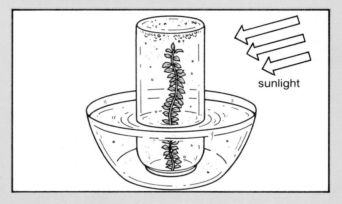

Stand the equipment on a sunny windowsill. Oxygen bubbles will soon appear and the oxygen will collect in the top of the jar.

8 Algae. Keep a jar of pond or lake water or a jar of rainwater on a sunny windowsill. See if any algae grow in the water. If they do, the water will go green. Look at some of this green water with a microscope. What do you see?

9 Study mallard ducks. Draw a large map of the area where you live or obtain a ready-made one. Glue the map onto a large sheet of cardboard. Make little flags from pins and pieces of colored sticky paper. Use the little flags to mark the ponds, lakes, gravel pits, clay pits, and other places where mallards can be found. Ask local people whether there are more or fewer mallards than there used to be. Why is this?

Watch some mallards carefully. See how they feed. Is a mallard a herbivore, a carnivore, or an omnivore? How do mallards swim, and take-off and land on water? How many eggs does a mallard lay? How big are they? How long is it before the ducklings are fully grown?

Make a list of the other water birds that share ponds and lakes with mallards. Do any of these birds attack the mallards? Do the mallards attack any other birds? If so, which?

10   Flatworms. Tie a small piece of raw liver on to the end of a length of thin string. Lower the liver into a pond. After an hour or two pull the liver out again. Can

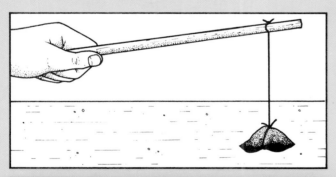

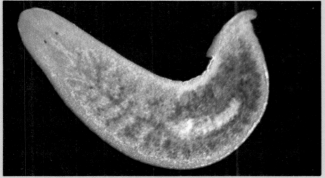

you see any tiny worms on it? These are called flatworms. Count how many there are on the piece of liver.

Can you catch most flatworms in shady parts of the pond or out in the open? Look at one of the flatworms carefully with a hand lens or magnifying glass. Draw it. Put all the flatworms back when you have finished with them.

11   Temporary ponds. Many small ponds are temporary. They are there only in wet weather. Temporary ponds include the water which collects in a hollow in a tree, puddles, and water-filled wheel ruts.

A water filled hollow in tree roots

Collect samples of water from one of these temporary ponds. Use a magnifying glass to see if you can find any living things in the water. How did these creatures reach the temporary pond? What happens to them if the pond dries up?

12   Keep a pond diary. Visit a pond regularly for a whole year and record the plants and animals (including birds) you see there. Keep a diary of your pond. Illustrate your entries with drawings or photographs.

Frogs

Springtime is a good time to see frogs. It is then that these animals go to ponds and ditches to lay their eggs. Frogs' eggs are laid in a mass of jelly and are called spawn. The spawn floats on the water. Before long each egg hatches into a tiny wriggling tadpole.

The newly hatched tadpoles breathe through gills on the sides of their heads. They eat small pieces of plant. After a time they begin to eat tiny water animals. Soon the tadpoles begin to grow hind legs. Shortly afterward the front legs appear. As the tadpoles grow older, their tails gradually disappear. The tadpoles have now become tiny frogs that breathe with lungs. It takes about 3 months for this to happen. Many thousands of tadpoles and young frogs are eaten by other animals. Those which do survive leave the pond in summer.

On land, frogs feed on worms, insects, grubs, spiders, and slugs. When winter comes, some of the frogs creep into holes in the ground. Others bury themselves in the mud at the bottom of ponds or ditches. They sleep, or hibernate, until the warmer weather returns. Then the fully grown ones go to the ponds where they were born to lay their eggs.

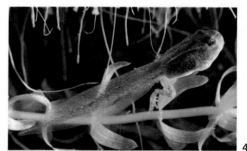

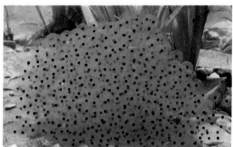

1. Frogs mating. 2. Frog spawn. 3. Newly hatched tadpoles. 4. Tadpole with hind legs emerging. 5. Young frog. The tail has not yet disappeared.

Toads

Common toad

Toad spawn

Toads are also common in ponds in spring. Toads look similar to frogs. But a toad's hind legs are shorter than those of a frog. And a toad's skin is rough and covered with warty pimples, whereas a frog's skin is smooth. Toads always walk, while frogs leap.

Toads lay their spawn in ponds from March onward. The jelly covered eggs are laid in double rows. The long strings of spawn hang amongst the water weeds in the pond. One toad may lay 7,000 eggs. Toad tadpoles grow up in the same way as frog tadpoles. Like their frog relatives, many toad tadpoles are eaten by fish, water birds, and other carnivores.

After they have laid their eggs, adult toads go back on land. There they hide away during the daytime. You can sometimes find a toad in a hole under tree roots or in a hedgebank. At dusk the toad leaves its hiding place to search for food. Toads eat worms, snails, woodlice, caterpillars, ants, beetles, flies, and other insects. The toad is an expert at catching insects. It watches its prey for a few seconds. Then it flicks out its tongue to catch the insect. Unlike our tongue, the tongue of a toad or frog is hinged at the front end.

In autumn, a toad creeps into a cozy burrow to hibernate until spring.

Newts

Many ponds have newts. Like frogs and toads, newts are amphibians. This means they spend part of their life on land and part in the water. Unlike frogs and toads, newts have long tails. Two kinds of newt live in North America. One newt is the California newt, which can be found in humid regions of western North America. The other newt is the red eft which can be found in eastern North America.

Male great crested newt

Left, common or smooth newt. *Below*, male palmate newt

In the early spring, newts enter the water to breed. The male newt has grown an enlarged fin. He carries out a fluttering dance in the water. This is his way of courting a female newt. Unlike frogs and toads, newts lay only one egg at a time. Each egg is protected by jelly. It is folded up on the leaf of a water plant. There the egg develops into a tadpole which looks something like a baby fish. It takes about 10 weeks for a newt tadpole to change into a newt.

Newt tadpole

At the end of the breeding season the adult newts leave the pond. They stay on the land until the next spring. By day they remain hidden in burrows or under stones and logs. At night they come out to feed on worms, slugs, and other small animals. In winter, newts hibernate in holes in the ground.

Dragonflies and damselflies

Above, two species of dragonfly

Dragonfly nymph with a small minnow

A damselfly

Dragonflies are large and handsome insects. Some are 2 to 3 inches long. All dragonflies hold their two pairs of wings outstretched when they are at rest. Dragonflies can fly very fast and hover in mid-air. They can even fly backward. They feed on flying insects that they catch with their legs and feet as they hurtle through the air. Dragonflies are called horse stingers, but dragonflies cannot sting humans or other animals.

Most female dragonflies lay their eggs in the water. A few kinds drill a hole in the stems or leaves of water plants and lay their eggs there. The eggs hatch into fierce-looking creatures called nymphs. The nymphs have powerful jaws. These are on a hinged flap called the mask. The nymph can shoot out its mask and grab any passing tadpole, small fish, or other small animal. It often takes 4 or 5 years for a nymph to turn into an adult dragonfly.

Damselflies are like small versions of dragonflies. They also have two pairs of transparent wings. But these are folded back along the body when the damselfly is at rest. Like dragonflies, damselflies are flying hunters, catching and eating other insects. Damselflies have a life cycle similar to that of dragonflies. Their eggs are laid in water and hatch into a nymph stage.

Water beetles and water bugs

Several kinds of water beetles live in ponds. The fiercest is the great diving beetle. It feeds on fish, tadpoles, and other small water creatures. The young or larvae of the great diving beetle are also fierce hunters. They are often called water tigers. They grow to be 2 or 2½ inches long. The larvae eat many tadpoles and small fish. Both the diving beetle and its larvae have to come to the surface of the water to breathe. The adult beetle traps air under its hard wing cases. Like all beetles, the great diving beetle can fly. It usually flies after dark, moving from one pond to another.

Although they look like beetles, water boatmen are really bugs. Bugs can only eat liquid food with their sucking, pointed mouthparts. Water boatmen swim rapidly through the water. They mainly swim upside down. Some people call them back swimmers. Water boatmen feed on the juices of tadpoles, small fish, and other small water creatures.

Great diving beetles, male in foreground

Larva of great diving beetle

Water striders are also water bugs. They spend most of their life striding across the surface of the water. Water striders use their shorter front legs to catch their food. They feed mainly on insects which fall in the water.

Left, Water strider. *Below*, water boatman

Caddis flies and water spiders

Adult caddis flies

Tubes made by caddis larvae

Right, Caddis fly larva. *Below*, A water spider in its underwater web

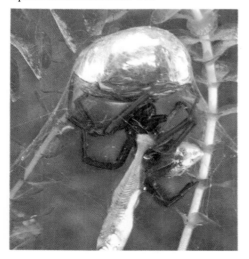

Another winged pond insect is the caddis fly. Adult caddis flies look rather like brown moths. They are not related to moths, though.

The caddis fly lays its eggs in or near water. The larvae which hatch from the eggs have a soft body. They protect themselves by making a tube around their bodies. Most caddis larvae make their tubes from sand grains or little pieces of plant material. Often the tubes are decorated with pieces of shell or stone. This makes it very hard for enemies of the caddis larvae to spot them. Most kinds of caddis larvae feed on water plants.

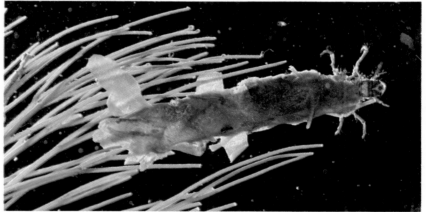

The water spider is the only spider which spends all its life underwater. It can even spin a web underwater. This web is a bell-shaped tube. Usually it is made between the leaves of water plants. The spider may make several of these webs. It uses them for feeding, resting, and laying its eggs. The water spider can't breathe air dissolved in the water. Instead it takes air bubbles from the surface and stores them in its webs. Water spiders prey on insects, freshwater shrimps, and even small fish.

Water snails

There are many kinds of water snails in a pond. Pond snails have brown or blackish-brown shells, coming to a point at one end. The shell covers most of the snail's soft body. When it moves, the snail glides along on its foot, which is a strip of muscle. A pond snail has two tentacles. These contain its eyes and other sense organs. Pond snails are herbivores, although some kinds will also feed on the dead remains of animals.

Ramshorn snails look rather different. Their shells form a flat spiral. They, too, eat mainly water plants. Pond snails and ramshorn snails lay eggs on the underside of the leaves of water plants. The eggs are protected in strips of stiff jelly. They hatch into tiny snails. As these feed and grow their shells grow with them.

Great pond snail

Ramshorn snail

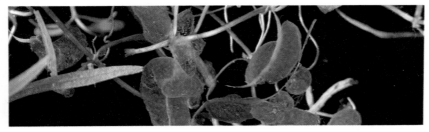

A water snail is protected by its coiled shell. However, swan mussels, which are related to water snails, have two large shells to protect them. Swan mussels are usually found half-buried in mud or sand. They feed by sucking in water through a short tube between the two shells. Any food particles in the water are sieved out by the swan mussel. Then the water is passed out through a second, longer tube. In one hour a swan mussel may pass 21 gallons of water through its body.

Left, Eggs of ramshorn snail

Swan mussel showing feeding tubes

No escape

Polluted pond

Pond used as a garbage dump

Water helps to protect pond plants and animals. It stops them from getting too hot or too cold. It enables them to drink, breathe, and to move about. Many pond animals can only feed and breed in water. Indeed most water plants and animals cannot survive anywhere else other than in a pond, lake, or ditch. The fish, leeches, water snails, nymphs, and larvae, for example, cannot survive out of water.

If a rabbit's burrow is destroyed, the rabbit can move to another field or wood. When a deer is in danger it can run away. If a pond is destroyed the water birds can fly to another pond. Some animals such as frogs, toads, and newts might get away. But there may not be another pond or ditch anywhere near that they can crawl to.

Most water animals cannot fly. They cannot escape when a pond dries up or is filled in. Nor can they escape if poisonous chemicals get into a pond or if garbage is dumped in it. Already many ponds, pond animals, and plants have been destroyed. We shall have to take great care of the ponds we have left.

Get to know your local pond

Cleaning a polluted pond

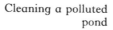

Do you remember?

(Look for the answers in the part of the book you have just been reading if you do not know them.)

1 What do we call frogs' eggs and the mass of jelly in which they are laid?

2 What do newly-hatched tadpoles feed on?

3 Where do frogs hibernate?

4 What are three ways in which toads are different from frogs?

5 What is toad spawn like?

6 How does the tongue of a frog or toad differ from a human tongue?

7 What is an amphibian?

8 How are the eggs of newts different from those of frogs or toads?

9 What do adult newts eat?

10 How many wings do dragonflies have, and how are they held when the insect is at rest?

11 Why might dragonflies have got the name horse stingers?

12 What is the young dragonfly called and what does it feed on?

13 How do damselflies differ from dragonflies?

14 How does the adult great diving beetle obtain air to breathe?

15 What is unusual about the way in which a water boatman swims?

16 Where do water striders spend most of their life?

17 How do caddis larvae protect themselves?

18 What does the water spider use its webs for?

19 What do most pond snails feed on?

20 How does the swan mussel obtain its food?

Things to do

1 **Make an underwater viewer.** Find a large tin to make an underwater viewer. Ask a grown-up to remove the top and bottom with a can opener. Carefully hammer down any sharp pieces. Cover the top and bottom rims of the tin with masking tape or duct tape.

Cover one end of the tin with plastic wrap. Fix this tightly with a rubber band.

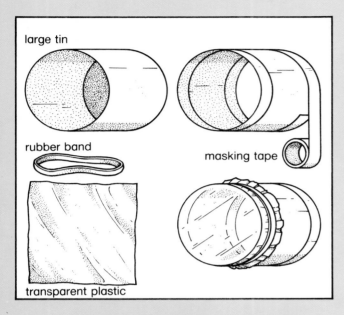

large tin

rubber band

masking tape

transparent plastic

Look at the spawn carefully with a hand lens or magnifying glass. What does each egg look like? Can you see the little black dots? These are the parts of the eggs which will grow into tadpoles.

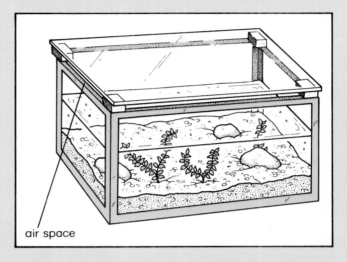

air space

Gently push the plastic-covered end of the viewer just below the surface of the water in a pond. Look through the open end to see what is happening under water. For best results work on a bright, sunny day. But avoid standing where you will cast a shadow on the area of water you wish to study.

Important: Use your viewer only in places where a grown-up says it is safe to do so, and ask a grown-up to stay with you until you have finished using your viewer.

2 Frog and toad spawn. Try to hatch some frog or toad spawn. Do not collect more than ten or twelve eggs.

Make a home for the spawn. Put some clean gravel in the tank or bowl and then plant some pieces of water weed. You will need some water from a pond or some rainwater. Do not use tap water unless it has been allowed to stand in the open for several days.

Draw the spawn every day. Do not forget to put the date on each picture. When the tadpoles have hatched, draw a picture of them. Watch how they feed on the pieces of water plant. Later, when their legs start to appear, the tadpoles will need animal food. Live water fleas and gnat and mosquito larvae are best. Very small pieces of raw lean meat or liver can also be given. However, these must not be left in the water for more than two or three hours, otherwise they will decay and pollute the water.

When do the tadpole's back legs appear? Do both front legs grow at the same time? When does the tadpole's tail start to shorten and disappear?

It is a good idea to let your tadpoles or young frogs go when the tail disappears. They then become difficult to feed properly in captivity. Let your tadpoles or frogs go free in a suitable pond, otherwise they will die.

Forty or fifty years ago frogs were very common animals. Now there are nowhere near as many frogs as there used to be. Why do you think this is?

3 Water snails. Keep two or three water snails in a large jar of pond water with some water plants. Watch how the snails feed. How do the snails move about inside the jar? Use a hand lens or magnifying glass to study the snails' muscles as they climb up the glass. What do you notice?

4 The eggs of water snails. Look carefully at the undersides of the leaves of water lilies and other water plants to find water snails' eggs. Collect a leaf which has eggs on it. Put the leaf in a white dish with water from the pond. Study the eggs with a hand lens or magnifying glass. How many eggs are there in one mass?

Keep the eggs in pond water. How many of them hatch out? What do the baby snails look like? How quickly do they grow?

5 A pond bottle garden. A pond is like a miniature world, where all the plants and animals' lives are linked by food chains.

Make a miniature pond in a large jar. Find the biggest clean jar that you can – a candy jar is ideal. Thoroughly wash some gravel and put a layer of it in the bottom of the jar. Then push a few sprigs of water weed (such as pondweed or hornwort) into the gravel. Gently fill the jar almost to the top with pond water.

Put two or three small herbivores in the jar. Small pond snails or ramshorn snails are good ones to try. Loosely fit the lid on the jar, and stand it near a window.

In the jar the water weeds provide food and oxygen for the snails. The snails breathe out air containing the gas carbon dioxide which the plants need to help make their food.

Your pond bottle garden should last for quite a long time without attention. Check it regularly, though, to see that the water stays clear and that it does not smell. If the water does start to smell, take the plants and animals back to a pond as soon as possible.

Ask your teacher if you can set up an aquarium where you can see how the lives of plants, herbivores, carnivores, and scavengers are linked together as they are in a real pond.

6   Gnats and mosquitoes. This is one activity with pond animals that everyone can do, wherever he or she lives.

In summer, look at the surface of still water for eggs of gnats or mosquitoes. They look like tiny rafts. Good places to find them are in the water which collects in hollow trees, upturned garbage can lids, forgotten buckets, as well as ponds and ditches.

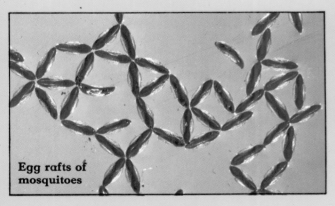

Egg rafts of mosquitoes

Keep some of the eggs *outside* in a jar of pond water or the stale water from a vase of flowers.

The eggs hatch into tiny larvae or wrigglers after a few days. Each larva changes into a pupa after about three weeks. An adult gnat or mosquito develops inside the pupa and flies away after the skin of the pupa has split open.

Study the various stages in the life history of the gnat or mosquito with a hand lens or magnifying glass. Keep a diary of what happens. Try to draw some of the stages in the life of the gnat or mosquito.

7   How leeches move. Leeches are common pond animals. Put a leech in a shallow dish of pond water. Look at the leech with a hand lens or magnifying glass. Draw a large picture of the leech.

Watch the leech to see how it moves. Draw a series of pictures to show how the animal uses its suckers.

Measure the leech when it is short and when it is stretched out. What is the difference between the two measurements?

8   Vertebrates and invertebrates. Scientists divide animals into two main groups. Many animals have a backbone inside their bodies. These are called vertebrates. Cows, dogs, cats, mice, chicken, and snakes are just a few of the animals which are vertebrates.

Ants, bees, wasps, flies, beetles, snails, woodlice, spiders, jellyfish, and crabs do not have a backbone inside their bodies. They are all invertebrates.

Make a table like this:

POND ANIMALS	
Vertebrates	Invertebrates
Mallard	Dragonfly
Stickleback	Swan mussel

Write down all the animals you know of or can find out about which live in or near ponds. Put their names in the correct column. In which column are there most animals? What do you notice about the general sizes of vertebrates and invertebrates?

9 A small garden pond. Ask permission to make a small pond in the yard. Choose an open part of the yard away from trees and hedges.

Dig a hole no more than 11 inches deep. Line the hole with a large bowl, or old stoneware sink (with the drain hole blocked), or with thick plastic sheeting as shown in the picture.

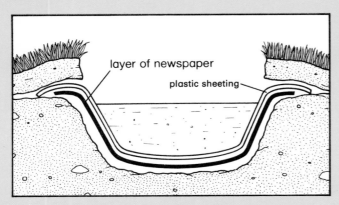

layer of newspaper

plastic sheeting

Fill the hole with rainwater or tapwater. Look at the pond carefully at least once a week. What animals and plants come to live in your pond? How do they get to your pond?

Do any other animals use your pond for drinking or bathing?

Keep a diary describing the changes that take place in your pond over a period of, say, a year.

Experiments to try

Do your experiments carefully. Write or draw what you have done and what happens. Say what you have learned. Compare your findings with those of your friends.

1 Which pond dries up first?

Which pond dries up first, a wide shallow one or a smaller deeper one?

What you need: A saucer and a clean paste jar.

What you do: Fill the paste jar to the top with water. Carefully empty this water into the saucer. Stand the saucer on a windowsill or shelf indoors. This is your wide, shallow pond.

Fill the paste jar to the top again with water. This is your smaller, deeper pond. Stand it by the side of the saucer of water.

What happens to the water after a day or so? Which dries up first? Why? Where has the water gone?

2 Do pond animals prefer dim light or bright light?

What you need: Some small water animals; pond water or rainwater; a long narrow plastic box; black paper; cloth or index card; saran wrap or transparent plastic; a desk lamp or flashlight; a plastic spoon and a small paint brush; a watch or clock.

What you do: Put 1 or 1½ inches of pond water or rain water in the plastic box. Cover exactly half of the box with black paper, black index card or black cloth.

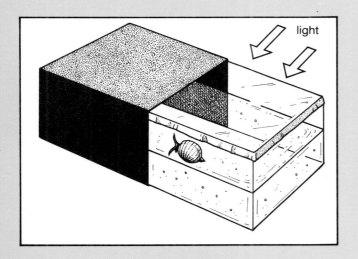

light

Put a small water animal, such as a pond snail, exactly in the middle of the box. Do not pick up fragile animals with your fingers. Scoop them up with the spoon and paint brush instead. Cover the box with saran wrap or transparent plastic, and quickly shine a flashlight or desk lamp onto the top of the box.

At the end of 10 minutes, see whether the snail is in the bright or the dimly lit part of the box.

Now do the experiment again with another snail of the same kind. Then do the experiment three more times with three more snails of the same kind.

Make a table on some paper, and record your results.

Now try the experiment with five more animals of another kind.

Do all animals of the same kind behave in the same way? Which animals prefer bright light and which prefer dim light?

3   How much food does a water snail eat in a day?

What you need: A plastic sandwich box; paper towel or filter paper; a large pond snail or ramshorn snail; a lettuce leaf; a piece of squared paper or graph paper; a pencil; pond water.

What you do: Two-thirds fill the sandwich box with clean pond water.

Lay the lettuce leaf on the squared paper and carefully draw around it.

Put the leaf under water in the sandwich box. Gently put the snail on it. Cover the box with a lid with small breathing holes in it, or with a piece of plastic in which small holes have been pierced. Leave the box in a quiet part of the room, away from the heaters and radiators, for 24 hours.

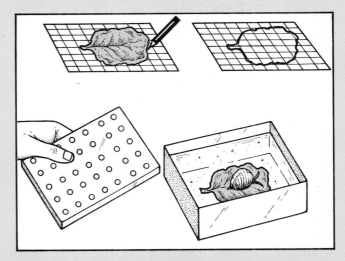

At the end of 24 hours carefully remove the leaf. Blot it gently with the filter paper or paper towel. Lay the leaf on the squared paper and mark out the pieces that have been eaten. Count how many squares of the leaf the snail has eaten.

Try the experiment again with other kinds of water snails and other pond herbivores. Try it with other kinds of leaves, including those of water weeds.

Which kind of pond herbivore eats the most lettuce leaf in 24 hours? Which kind of leaf is the most popular as a food for pond herbivores?

4 Why is the water strider able to walk on water?

What you need: A clean jam jar or glass; a piece of tissue paper; a small sewing needle; a hand lens or magnifying glass.

What you do: Fill the jar or glass with cold tap water. Float a small piece of tissue paper (about the size of a quarter) on the water. Carefully rest the sewing needle on the tissue paper.

Watch carefully and see what happens when the tissue paper becomes waterlogged and sinks. Try to avoid knocking the glass or the table, and carefully look at the surface of the water with the hand lens or magnifying glass. What is the needle doing?

What have you learned about the surface of the water?

5 How does duckweed multiply?

As we saw on page 4, duckweed is a small plant which floats on the surface of ponds. Each duckweed plant looks like a leaf, with tiny roots hanging down from it. How does a duckweed plant multiply?

What you need: A few duckweed plants; pondwater or rainwater; clean jam jars.

What you do: Two-thirds fill a jam jar with pondwater or rainwater. Float one duckweed plant on the surface of the water. Stand the jar on a sunny windowsill.

Once every week, examine the plant carefully with a hand lens or magnifying glass. Do not touch the duckweed plant. Draw the plant each week. Every week also record how many duckweed plants there are in your jar. Make a graph of your results. Put the numbers of duckweed plants along the side of your graph and the number of weeks since you started the experiment at the bottom.

If the water in the jar begins to dry up add more, but try not to disturb the plants.

Do the experiment again. This time use two jars and two duckweed plants. Put one in a warm, sunny place and the other in a cool place. What differences do you see between the two jars after a week or two?

6 How long can water birds stay underwater?

What you need: A stop watch or a watch with a second hand; a notebook and pen and pencil. Work in the public park or the yard where there is a pond or lake with water birds on it.

What you do: Choose a species of water bird which dives for its food. Good ones to try include tufted ducks, coots, great crested grebes, or little grebes.

When one of your chosen birds goes underwater, time how long it is before the bird reappears. Do this for as many dives as you can. Make a graph of your results like this. Find out the average length of time the bird stays underwater on each dive.

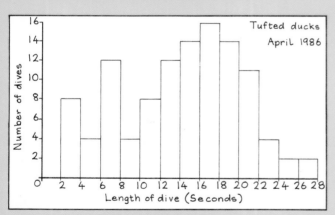

Now do the same thing with other species of diving water birds. Which species can stay underwater the longest?

7 How small a piece of pondweed is needed to make a new plant?

Pondweed does not produce seeds. It spreads because pieces that are broken off the plant grow roots. What is the smallest piece of pondweed which will form a new plant?

What you need: Some pondweed; five clean jam jars; a sharp knife; a ruler.

What you do: Take five leafy shoots of the pondweed. Cut one so that there is 2 inches of stem, together with the growing tip. Cut four others in the same way, but making them 1½, 1, ¾, ½ inches long. Do not let the pondweed dry out while you are doing this.

Half fill each of the five jars with cold tap water, rainwater, or pond water. Place one of the leafy shoots in each.

Stand all five jars in a row on a sunny windowsill. Label the jars with the date and the length of the leafy shoot they contain.

Look at the shoots each week for four weeks. Which of the leafy shoots grows roots? Measure the shoots at the end of the four weeks. Which has grown the most?

What is the smallest piece of pondweed which will grow into a new plant? Do the experiment again but cut the growing tip off each shoot. Does this make any difference to the results?

Glossary

Here are the meanings of some words which you might have met for the first time in this book.

Algae: very simple green plants without stems, leaves, or flowers.

Amphibian: a cold-blooded animal, such as a frog, toad, or newt, that can live in water and on land.

Bug: insects which suck up liquid food with their pointed mouthparts.

Carnivore: flesh-eating animals; animals that prey on other animals.

Evaporate: when a liquid such as water gradually changes to a vapor or gas, we say it has evaporated.

Food chain: the way in which living things are linked together by energy in the form of food. Plants obtain their energy from sunlight. They are eaten by herbivores which, in turn, are eaten by carnivores.

Herbivore: an animal which feeds on plants.

Hibernate: to sleep during the winter.

Invertebrate: an animal which does not have a backbone inside its body. Most invertebrate animals are quite small and many live in water.

Lake: a large area of water surrounded by land.

Larva: the feeding stage in the life of an insect which comes from the egg. Maggots, caterpillars, and grubs are examples of larvae.

Nymphs: the name given to the young of certain insects, such as dragonflies, damselflies and mayflies.

Permanent pond: a pond which always has water in it.

Pond: a small body of still water.

Scavengers: animals which feed on dead plants, dead animals, and animal droppings.

Spawn: the eggs of fishes and other egg-laying water animals such as frogs and toads.

Tadpole: the young stage of a frog, toad, or newt, that hatches from an egg.

Temporary pond: a pond that has water in it for only a short period of time before it dries up.

Vertebrate: an animal that has a backbone inside its body.

Acknowledgments

The publishers would like to thank the following for permission to reproduce transparencies:

Heather Angel: front cover (center left), p. 3 (bottom right), p. 4 (inset). p. 6 (top and center); p. 10 (top and center), p. 17 (center), p. 18 (top, center and bottom), p. 19 (top and 2nd from bottom), p. 20 (top, center and bottom), p. 21 (top, center left and right), p. 22 (top, center left and right), p. 23 (bottom left), p. 30 (right), back cover (bottom and top); BIOFOTOS/Jeremy Thomas: p. 19 (2nd from top); Richard Crawford: p. 2 (top middle and right, bottom), p. 3 (bottom left), p. 12 (bottom right), p. 15 (top right); Eric and David Hosking: front cover (top right), p. 3 (center), p. 8 (top center, bottom left and right), p. 9 (top inset); Hosking/WS Pitt: p. 7 (top and bottom); Terry Jennings: front cover (bottom left and right), p. 2 (top left, center right), p. 3 (top), p. 9 (center, bottom and bottom inset), p. 17 (top), p. 18 (center left), p. 19 (bottom), p. 20 (bottom, left); Frank Lane/Leo Batten: p. 23 (bottom right); Frank Lane/W Howes: p. 7 (center); Frank Lane/Steve McCutcheon: p. 23 (center): Oxford Scientific Films; OSF/GI Bernard: p. 16 (2nd from top, center, 2nd from bottom, bottom), p. 22 (bottom), p. 27 (right); OSF/JAL Cooke: p. 21 (bottom); OSF/Peter Parks: p. 15 (bottom right); OSF/Barrie E Watts: p. 16 (top); Science Photo Library/Jerry Mason: p. 23 (top); Shell UK Photographic Library: p. 27 (left).

Illustrated by Paula L Cox   David Eaton   Edward McLachlan   Cathy Wood

Index